AXOLOTL
CARE MADE
EASY

A Family-Friendly Guide for Axolotl Lovers - Discover Together How to Nurture Your Little Water Buddy and Ensure a Happy Growth Journey

CAMILLE PERRY

Table of Content

INTRODUCTION

Hey there, water adventurers and future axolotl pals! If you've picked up this book, it's clear you're ready to dive into a spectacular journey with one of the most extraordinary creatures from the underwater world - the remarkable Axolotl!

You might be scratching your head, wondering, "What on earth is an Axolotl?" Well, we're super excited that you've asked! Axolotls aren't your typical pets like dogs, cats, or even goldfish. No, these critters are like magic, seeming to swim right out of a fantastical tale and into our lives.

Axolotls (say it with me: ax-oh-lot-ul) are one-of-a-kind salamanders that never really grow up. They're like the "Peter Pan" of the animal kingdom because they stay in their youthful form their whole lives, something that brainy scientists call 'neoteny.' Isn't that just the coolest thing?

But hold on to your hats, because it gets even better. They have a superpower that would make even a superhero green with envy - they can grow back parts of their bodies! Picture this: losing a tail and then, poof, growing it back again. How wild is that?

By now, you're probably thinking, "Golly, Axolotls sound like the best pets ever!" And you'd be spot on. These grinning, frilly-gilled, water-loving pals are full of surprises and can bring oodles of happiness into your world. They're a breeze to take care of, making them just the ticket for young animal enthusiasts like you. And they're sure to make you the talk of the town - not everyone can say they have a pet that looks like it stepped out of a Pokémon game, right?

But like all pets, axolotls need our TLC - that's Tender Loving Care. They depend on us to make a cozy home for them and to keep them healthy and chipper.

That's where this book comes in: 'Axolotl Care Made Easy: A Family-Friendly Guide for Axolotl Lovers - Discover Together How to Nurture Your Little Water Buddy and Ensure a Happy Growth Journey.' This is your treasure map to the enchanting world of axolotls.

We'll explore the world of axolotls together, learning what tasty treats they like to eat, how to set up the perfect tank, and even how to understand their moods and behaviors. Most importantly, we'll learn the ins and outs of axolotl care to make sure your little water buddy is always feeling top-notch.

So, are you ready to set sail on this underwater voyage? We hope so, because your axolotl can't wait to meet you. Let's plunge in and make some waves in the thrilling world of axolotls together!

GETTING TO KNOW YOUR AXOLOTL

Axolotls might look a bit like fish, but guess what? They're part of the amphibian family! These unusual creatures live their whole lives underwater. People sometimes call them "Mexican walking fish" because of the way they look and move. Axolotls have some truly amazing and special traits that make them stand out in the animal kingdom. Let's dive in and find out more about these magical creatures!

A Touch of Magic: The Power of Regeneration

Imagine if you could grow back a tooth you lost, or if a scraped knee healed in just one night. That'd be pretty cool, right? Well, guess what! Axolotls can do something even more fantastic. They can grow back entire body parts!

Yes, you heard that right. Axolotls have a superpower that could make even superheroes green with envy. They can regenerate, meaning they can grow back parts of their bodies that get injured or lost. And we're not just talking about tails or legs. They can even grow back hearts, spines, and parts of their brains!

You might be asking, "How on earth do they do that?" The truth is, scientists are still trying to figure out all the details. But here's what we know: when an axolotl gets hurt, its body springs into action to fix itself. The cells near the injured area start to change, forming a special group of cells called a "blastema." Think of the blastema like a construction crew, building a new body part bit by bit until it's good as new!

And here's an even more amazing fact: if an axolotl loses an arm or a leg, it doesn't just grow back any old limb. The axolotl knows exactly what part is missing and grows back the right one every time. If it loses a front leg, it grows back a front leg, not a back leg or a tail. How incredible is that?

The ability of the axolotl to regenerate is like a magical trick from nature. It's like a real-life phoenix rising from the ashes, perfectly whole again. The more we learn about these incredible creatures, the more we can marvel at the wonders and mysteries of the animal kingdom.

Forever Young: The Amazing Axolotl

Have you ever wished you could stay young forever? Well, axolotls do just that! They look like babies their whole lives. This is because they're "neotenic," which means they grow up without ever losing their youthful features. They stay in their baby stage for life, except for one part that does grow up: their reproductive organs. This helps them to have babies of their own and continue their species.

In simpler words, neoteny is like being a kid who never grows up. Most salamanders start to breathe air and live on land when they grow up, turning their gills into lungs. But our friend, the axolotl, stays in the water, breathing through the same gills from babyhood all the way to adulthood.

Because they stay in their baby stage, axolotls' teeth never fully develop. They have to use a suction system to eat their food. They keep their feathery gills and long dorsal fin, even when they're all grown up.

Most amphibians start their lives in water, breathing through gills. When they grow up, they change their body shape and size and lose their gills. This transformation is called metamorphosis. But axolotls don't do this. They're missing a hormone needed to make thyroxine, which is what animals need to go through metamorphosis. Because they don't have this hormone, axolotls keep their gills and live in the water their whole lives, even when they're all grown up and ready to have babies. This is all thanks to their unique genetic makeup.

So, while many amphibians like salamanders eventually move onto land, axolotls grow up without ever going through metamorphosis. They keep their feathery external gills and live underwater for their entire lives.

Sometimes, after eating, axolotls keep their mouths open for a few seconds, making them look like they're smiling. This, along with their forever-young looks, makes them very appealing to pet owners. Some axolotls even seem to have slightly open mouths all the time, making them look like they're always smiling. But don't be fooled! It's not because they're always happy, it's just the way they look. This "smiling" appearance might make a pet owner feel hopeful, but remember, it's just an illusion!

Unraveling the Mystery: Is My Axolotl a Boy or a Girl?

One curiosity you might want to figure out is the sex of your axolotl. How can you tell if your little buddy is a male or a female? Well, let's dive into this mystery!

As axolotls grow, they start to show some differences that can help us guess if they are boys or girls. Keep in mind, this isn't always easy, and even experts sometimes get it wrong, so don't worry if you can't tell right away!

Male axolotls usually have a slimmer body and a wider tail, while females tend to be a bit chunkier with shorter, plumper tails. Boys also have a bump, called a cloaca, near their tails, which girls don't have. But here's the tricky part - sometimes, young girls can have this bump too, and only lose it as they grow older.

So, the best way to know for sure is to watch your axolotl grow and keep an eye out for these changes. And remember, whether your axolotl turns out to be a boy or a girl, it will still be the same adorable, interesting creature that you fell in love with!

Munch, Munch, Munch

Axolotls are little water monsters when it comes to food. They'll chow down on just about anything they can find, like tiny fish, bugs, snails, worms, and other small water creatures. That's why we call them carnivores.

In your tank or aquarium at home, they'll happily eat special axolotl pellets or fish meal, brine shrimp, tiny pieces of beef liver, and earthworms. When they're young or if they're really hungry, axolotls can get a little naughty and nibble on their tank mates. But don't worry! Remember their superpower? They can easily grow back any lost body parts.

Axolotls are forever babies (scientists call this neotenic), so they don't have proper teeth. They suck up their food instead. While they don't need to eat every day, they'll happily munch on anything you give them - be it fish, worms, or bugs. Sadly, in the wild, because of new water bullies in their home, our little water buddies are having a tough time finding enough to eat, and their numbers are dropping fast.

Breathing with Frilly Gills

You know how fish breathe underwater through gills, right? Well, axolotls do too, but their gills are a bit different. They're on the outside! They look like fancy feathers sticking out from the sides of their head. And that's not the only cool thing about them. Axolotls also have a tail fin that starts right behind their head and goes all the way to the end of their tail.

Most young water animals have gills, but as they grow up, these gills turn into lungs. Not for our forever-baby axolotls, though! They keep their frilly gills all their life because of their special feature called neoteny. Plus, their gills are super gills, helping them take in more oxygen than other water animals. And to protect these awesome gills, they've got four little slits underneath that keep out any nasty bits of dirt or debris.

A Giant Puzzle of DNA

Axolotls are one of the champions in the DNA game. They have the second-longest DNA base sequences among all creatures on Earth, with 32 billion DNA bases. That's ten times more than humans! This makes it a giant puzzle for scientists to sequence, but it's a challenge they're excited about.

Why are they so interested? Well, if they can solve this puzzle, they could discover how axolotls use their cells to do their amazing healing trick. They've already found two special genes that help axolotls regenerate, and they're eager to find more.

Because of their superpowers and unique DNA, researchers love working with axolotls. The Smithsonian even says they're "basically the white mice of amphibians, thanks to their unique genetic profile and their potential to unlock the secrets of evolution and regeneration." Isn't that just amazing?

The Dance of Love: Axolotl Style

Once axolotls grow up, they start looking for other axolotls to become friends with - special friends. This usually happens when they're about six months old, ready for a big step in their life. The boys start the search for the girls, drawn by a special scent that the girls release called pheromones.

Once they find each other, the axolotls do a special dance, a bit like the 'Hula', but this one is unique to them. This isn't just any dance though, it's their own special way of saying, "Hey, I like you." They rub together and move in a playful dance, rolling around in the water, twirling in a dance-off that's as unique as they are.

After the dance, the female axolotl lays about 100 to 300 eggs. She carefully tucks them onto water plants or rocks where they're safe from hungry creatures who might want to gobble them up. In the wild, this special dance happens just once a year, but when they live in a tank or aquarium, they might dance more often.

Once the eggs are laid, the mom and dad axolotl's job is done. After about 10 to 14 days, the little baby axolotls hatch and start to swim all by themselves, ready to explore their watery world. Isn't nature amazing?

Fun Facts and Features

Axolotls are truly amazing creatures. They start to grow up between 18 to 27 months, all the while living in the water. During this time, they can stretch out to anywhere from 15 to 45 centimeters (6 to 18 inches) long!

You might be surprised to know that when axolotls are very young and can't find any other food, they might nibble on their brothers or sisters. But don't worry! Any nibbled bits grow right back, just like magic.

Axolotls come in many colors. The wild ones shine in a golden color, mixed with green, brown, and black. This helps them blend in with their watery surroundings, keeping them safe from any animals that might want to eat them.

One of the coolest things about axolotls is their "frilly" gills that stick out from the sides of their heads. These gills, along with a fin that stretches from the back of their head all the way down to their tail, help them breathe and move around in the water. Unlike other animals, axolotls keep their gills their whole lives!

Axolotls have wide heads with tiny eyes on top that don't have any lids. Even though their eyesight isn't the best, they're still great at spotting changes in light and movement.

Their skin is smooth and a bit slimy, usually dark from brown to black. Some even have white or pink spots, making them even more unique. Their mouth opens in a horizontal slit and is designed to suck in food rapidly. They have small, rudimentary teeth used primarily for grasping rather than chewing prey. This suction feeding method is ideal for their underwater habitat, allowing them to feed on a variety of small creatures like worms, small fish, and crustaceans.

Axolotls have four legs, each with long, thin fingers, and an even longer tail that helps them swim and change direction easily. The tail can also be used to hold onto things, almost like a fifth hand!

Last but not least, axolotls have four slits under their gills that help keep their food from going the wrong way. With all these features, it's easy to see why axolotls are such incredible creatures.

The Colorful World of Axolotls

The Amazing Spectrum of Axolotl Colors Did you know that the world of axolotls is a vibrant one, bursting with a dazzling array of colors? Yep, it's true! This is all thanks to their amazing genes that paint them in different hues and patterns. Most axolotls in the wild rock a brown or black color, peppered with specks of gold or olive. But here's the part that'll make your jaw drop - axolotls, like their salamander relatives, can actually alter their skin color to merge with their environment. It's as if they have a superpower—camouflage!

Axolotls are found in a variety of colors. Common ones include pink, brown, or black, often dusted with gold or olive specks. This unique chameleon-like ability to morph their color and blend underwater helps them evade predators or sneak up on prey. It's like they have a secret costume, making them even more lovable and appealing as pets. Some axolotls sport golden speckles, others are white, black, or even glow-in-the-dark!

And it's not just their bodies - even their gills flaunt different colors, adding to their distinctiveness. This is why axolotls have become such a hit as pets - their looks and traits are truly one-of-a-kind.

These days, humans breed axolotls in aquariums for a variety of reasons, spanning from commercial to scientific. Once teetering on the brink of extinction, careful breeding has now gifted us with a wide array of axolotl variations, showcasing different shapes, sizes, and colors. This process, known as "artificial selection," lets pet owners design their dream axolotl. Can you believe there are over 20 different kinds of axolotls?

So, whether you fancy a pink one, a black one with golden speckles, or something totally out-of-the-box, there's an axolotl out there that's your perfect match. The axolotl world is a kaleidoscope of color, ripe for exploration!

Let's take a look at some of the mesmerizing colorations of Axolotls:

1. The Majestic White Albino Axolotl

Have you ever come across a white axolotl? They're the most common pet axolotls, celebrated for their unique hue. These axolotls sport a pristine white body, striking red gill filaments, and eyes that can be pink or white.

But why are they white? It's because they churn out less of a pigment called melanin, which shields them from harmful UV light and adds color to their skin. These albino axolotls also have reduced pigments in their eyes, making them highly sensitive to light. Isn't that intriguing?

2. The Eye-catching Leucistic Axolotl

The leucistic axolotl is another extraordinary type. These axolotls wear skin that's almost transparent and gills that are a fiery red color. Their eyes are a deep, penetrating black. Often, they are mistaken for albino axolotls, but there's a world of difference between them.

While albinos lack just one pigment, melanin, leucistic axolotls are missing almost all skin pigments. That's why their skin is nearly transparent! There's also a unique variant of leucistic axolotl, the speckled leucistic, which has translucent skin decorated with green, brown, or black specks. It's as if they're wearing their own one-of-a-kind pattern!

3. The Uncommon Piebald Axolotl

Ever heard of a piebald axolotl? These little guys are super special and quite hard to find. Piebald axolotls showcase a partial leucistic morph, meaning they have spots or patches on their skin. The patches can be dark green or black, adding contrast to their see-through skin.

Most of the spots appear on their face and back, but sometimes you might spot a few on their sides and legs. However, they're different from speckled leucistic axolotls. Piebalds are adorned with more spots scattered across their bodies, creating a unique and attractive pattern that sets them apart.

So there you have it! The world of axolotls is as colorful as a rainbow, full of unique and fascinating creatures, each one more captivating than the last. Whether you're a fan of the pristine albinos, the transparent leucistics, or the uniquely patterned piebalds, there's an axolotl waiting to become your new best friend!

4. The Glittering Golden Albino Axolotl

Have you ever seen a golden axolotl? They are one of the most common artificial colors for these amazing creatures. Golden albino axolotls have a beautiful skin that shines like gold. Their eyes can be white, pink, or even yellow!

One special thing about golden albinos is that they have reflective patches on their bodies. These patches can make them look even more dazzling. And guess what? As they grow, their color can change from white to yellow and even to a radiant orange gold. Isn't that incredible?

When golden albino axolotls are born, they may look similar to standard albino axolotls. But as they grow into adults, they become quite different. This type of axolotl is the result of missing all other pigments except for yellow and gold. That's what gives them their unique and stunning appearance!

5. The Fascinating Copper Axolotl

Heard about the copper axolotl? It's a relatively uncommon axolotl type that sports a light gray-green body with a sprinkling of copper-colored flecks across its skin. Can you imagine just how gorgeous that must look? These axolotls showcase an intriguing mix of features. Their eyes are a muted gray, and their gills are a blend of gray and red. This unique combination is the result of restricted melanin and pigments in their skin. Copper axolotls are commonly found in the United States and Australia, but they can also be discovered in other countries. When bred with other axolotl types, they can create truly mesmerizing combinations!

6. The Enigmatic Black Melanoid Axolotl

The black melanoid axolotl is one of the most sought-after color variations of axolotls worldwide. Discovered in 1961, this axolotl type has skin pigments that can produce a range of colors from deep green to pitch black. How fantastic is that? Black melanoid axolotls have dark purple gills and a belly in shades of soft gray or purple. Some might appear quite similar to the wild-type axolotls, except they lack the golden iris. In some ways, they are the polar opposites of the albino axolotls. These black beauties, with their unique and striking appearance, are adored globally!

7. The Beguiling Lavender Axolotl

Picture an axolotl with a light silvery purple hue. That's the enchanting lavender axolotl for you! These axolotls radiate a special kind of charm. Their gills are a blend of gray and red, and their eyes are black, which can sometimes shift to green or gray as they age. The body of a lavender axolotl is covered in spots, earning it the nickname "silver Dalmatian axolotl." It's not easy to find these axolotls, and they can be quite pricey. But one look at their stunning color combo, and you'll comprehend why they are so coveted!

8. The Spectacular Firefly Axolotl

Now for something truly unique and somewhat contentious—the firefly axolotl! This color morph features a wild-type axolotl with a dark hue, but its tail is albino and it can glow in the dark under a black light. Isn't that just mind-blowing? The glow effect is triggered by a special protein known as green fluorescent protein, which originates from a jellyfish. Scientists introduced this protein into the axolotl to study its resistance to cancer. It's an uncommon and utterly captivating variation.

Axolotl's Tough Times in the Wild

Ever wonder about the lives of axolotls in their natural environment? These intriguing amphibians are exclusive to a tiny part of Mexico, and sadly, their numbers are on the decline. Imagine living in an area smaller than four square miles!

Our axolotl pals face numerous hurdles, from pollution and invasive species to human activities. Their homes, the canals of Mexico, are frequently drained or polluted with harmful substances, making their survival an uphill battle. Toxic chemicals and household waste have contaminated the residual water, creating an unsafe environment for these delightful creatures.

To add to their woes, invasive species like tilapia and carp have been introduced, competing fiercely with axolotls for food and resources. Picture this: having to share everything with newcomers who fancy the same menu as you do? It's tough for the axolotls, indeed!

Regrettably, axolotls are also being captured and traded as pets, particularly in the USA. Their unique features and regeneration abilities have sparked curiosity. While their study by scientists and researchers has aided their survival to an extent, they continue to face threats in their homeland.

Alarmingly, scientists estimate that the axolotl population has plunged by approximately 90% since 2009. In 2015, they were even believed to be extinct in the lakes of Mexico, though miraculously, one was found a week later. The rapid expansion of tourism, residential structures, and pollution from agriculture and industry have deeply scarred the axolotl population.

However, not all hope is lost. The Mexican government and numerous non-profit organizations are working tirelessly to safeguard these captivating creatures. They're devoted to reviving freshwater bodies and promoting ecotourism to observe these fascinating salamanders in their natural settings. Every contribution matters!

Conservationists are resorting to creative solutions to assist the axolotls. One such promising project involves constructing "Chinamapas." These man-made floating islands, composed of lake mud, aquatic plants, and logs, function as filters to purify the polluted water. By curtailing the population of harmful species, the water level can be restored, providing a more suitable habitat for our axolotl companions.

Though the exact number of axolotls remaining in the wild remains unknown, these conservation efforts are making a positive impact. It's heartening to witness scientists and farmers joining forces to protect these one-of-a-kind creatures. Together, we can secure a brighter future for axolotls and conserve their natural habitat for future generations. Let's rally behind our delightful aquatic friends!

SETTING UP YOUR AXOLOTL'S HOME

So, you're getting ready to welcome a new water buddy into your life? That's absolutely axo-some! But before you bring your new axolotl home, there are a few important things you need to know about setting up their aquatic crib. After all, we want to make sure your axolotl feels happy and comfy in its new home.

The right tank and equipment

Your axolotl is going to need a tank, but not just any tank! You see, these cool critters can grow pretty big - up to 14 inches long, although most of them like to chill around the 9-inch mark. That's about as long as a school ruler! So, a 20-gallon tank, which is 24 inches long and 12 inches wide, should be your starting point for an adult axolotl.
Your axolotl might feel all squashed up and worried in a smaller tank, and that's not fun for you or them! "But hang on a minute," you may think, "my axolotl is only a teeny little guy right now, only about 4-5 inches long!" Well, sure, you can start with a 10-gallon tank. Just remember, these adorable creatures grow up fast! So, plan ahead and be ready to move them to a bigger tank as your axolotl starts to stretch out. Also, a 10-gallon tank is the smallest you'll need to kick off a healthy nitrogen cycle, which is mega important for keeping your axolotl cheerful and thriving.

Now, axolotls might look like they're the life of the party, but in reality, they enjoy their own company. This is even more true when they're young because little axolotls can get somewhat... erm... nippy with each other. So, if you're bringing home more than one axolotl, it's best to give them their own spaces until they're about 3 to 4 inches long. You can do this by using an aquarium divider or even making one yourself. It's like giving each axolotl its own private bedroom in the tank!

And what about introducing your axolotl to a new tank buddy? Just keep in mind, axolotls are inquisitive little munchers, and if they see something that might fit in their mouth, they might just decide to take a little nibble.This could lead to some axolotl drama if you have axolotls of different sizes in the same tank. So, if you're planning on having more than one axolotl in a tank, make sure they're about the same size. And to keep the peace, try feeding them at opposite ends of the tank to make sure everyone gets their fair share of dinner.

These water buddies need some space to wiggle, waggle, and swim about. So, it's super important to pick the right sized tank. Here's a quick guide to help you:

- For one axolotl, you're going to need a tank that's at least 24 inches long.
- Got a pair of axolotls? Then you'll need a tank that's 36 inches long.
- If you're planning to have three axolotls, go for a tank that's 48 inches long.

Let's put it this way, kiddos, axolotls like having their space, a bit like you when you don't want to share your toys. They're not too keen on sharing their home with different types of animals, like fish or snails. You see, axolotls are quite curious and tend to munch on anything they come across - they're a bit like cookie monsters of the underwater world!

So, think twice before you get a new pet fish or snail thinking they'd make great pals with your axolotl. You might end up with an unexpected seafood feast for your axolotl. And it's not just a one-way street either. Fish, those little rascals, might mistake an axolotl's fancy gills for a scrumptious snack.

All in all, it's a good idea to let your axolotl have its own little kingdom, unless of course, you're bringing in another axolotl of the same size. Then, they might just hit it off!

Now, to make your axolotl's home truly comfy, you'll need a few essential pieces of equipment:

Aquarium Tank: Imagine this as your axolotl's very own bedroom. A 20-gallon tank is just the right size for a single axolotl, giving it plenty of room to move around. Axolotls like to go on little underwater adventures, so a long, rectangular tank is perfect. It's like their personal playground, with lots of space to swim and discover new things.

Filter System: Axolotls can be a bit like us after a big party - they leave a bit of a mess. So, a top-notch filter is needed to keep their water sparkling clean. Canister filters or sump filters are brilliant choices as they can handle all the leftovers from your axolotl's meals. The trick is to find a filter that can clean the tank's water at least four times an hour. But be gentle! We don't want a filter that makes the water move too fast. Axolotls have sensitive gills that might get upset if the water is too rough.

Chiller and Thermometer: Axolotls are cool little dudes, literally! They enjoy lounging in chilly water, so we need to keep the water temperature just right, between 59-65°F. Think of the aquarium chiller as your axolotl's personal AC, maintaining the perfect cool for their tank. And don't forget a thermometer - it's like their very own weatherman, letting us know if the water temperature needs adjusting.

Lighting: Just like us, axolotls need a bit of day and night to feel happy. But they're not big fans of bright lights - it's like when you have to wake up super early, and the sunlight is just too much. So, let's keep the lights soft and gentle, using a low-wattage light or even a screen to dim the brightness. That way, your axolotl will feel just right!
Here's a fun fact: Axolotls don't need UVB light because they get all their vitamins from their food. So, we don't need to worry about UVB lights at all - in fact, they could even be bad for our water buddies.
We should aim to replicate a normal day-night cycle, just like in nature. A timer can help with this. Ideal is a 12-hour light cycle and 12-hour dark cycle. LED lights are a great option for this, as they don't give off much heat (which could warm up the water too much), and you can adjust how bright they are. If the tank is in a room with natural light and it's not too bright, you might not even need extra lighting. Just remember, axolotls love a gentle glow, not a spotlight!

Substrate: You know, axolotls don't actually need a substrate, but if you want to add some, make sure it's smooth and rounded to keep your axolotls safe. Think of it like their carpet - we don't want it to be prickly! Sand or fine gravel can work well.

Water Testing Kit: Testing the water regularly is like giving your axolotl a health check. It helps us make sure the water has the right levels of ammonia, nitrite, nitrate, and pH. Here's what we're aiming for to keep our axolotls happy and healthy:

- Ammonia (NH_3): 0 parts per million (ppm)
- Nitrites (NO_2^-): 0 ppm
- Nitrates (NO_3^-): should be kept below 20 ppm.
- pH: the ideal is a value between 7.4 and 7.8. However, they can tolerate a range between 6.5 and 8.0

Water Conditioner: Just like you wouldn't want to swim in a pool full of chlorine, axolotls don't like it in their water. That's where a water conditioner comes in. It gets rid of chlorine and any other nasties that might be in the tap water.

Hiding Spots and Plants: Everyone needs a place to hide sometimes, and axolotls are no different. Giving them hiding spots and plants to explore keeps them entertained. Just make sure any decorations are smooth and rounded to keep your axolotl safe. Live plants are an excellent choice, as they can help clean the water and give your axolotl a bit of extra oxygen.

Create a suitable environment

To make sure our axolotl buddies are as happy as can be, we need to create the perfect home for them. This means getting the temperature just right, making sure the water in their tank is clean and clear, and keeping everything in balance. So, let's dive in and discover how to set up the ultimate axolotl pad!

Temperature

Just like Goldilocks, axolotls like their water not too hot, not too cold, but just right. As these guys are originally from chilly lakes, they prefer their water to be around 59-65°F. If the water gets over 72°F, that's like a heatwave for our axolotls and it's not good for them. That's why we need an aquarium thermometer, which is like their very own weather station.

One of the best ways to keep things cool is to use an aquarium chiller. This is like a mini fridge for the tank, making sure the temperature stays perfectly cool for your axolotl.

Choosing a chiller can be a bit like picking out a new pair of shoes - you gotta find the one that fits just right! This isn't about style though, it's all about the size of your tank. Chillers come in all sorts of sizes, and they're usually measured in horsepower (HP) or British Thermal Units

(BTUs). So, you'll want to make sure you get one that matches your tank size.

Now, there are two main types of chillers you can consider: refrigerated chillers and thermoelectric chillers. Refrigerated chillers are a bit pricier but really good at cooling the water. They work with a compressor and coolant system to keep the temperature just right. On the other hand, thermoelectric chillers are a bit cheaper, and while they're not quite as powerful, they do a good job of moving heat away from the water.

Okay, so you've chosen your chiller. What's next? Well, you'll have to connect it to your tank's filtration system. This will keep your water nice and cool as it circulates around the tank, preventing it from becoming too hot. Don't worry, your chiller should come with instructions to help you get set up. Just follow them carefully, and your tank will be chill in no time!

By using an aquarium chiller, you're giving your axolotl the best care possible and creating a home where they can really thrive.

While an aquarium chiller is a pretty cool piece of kit (literally!) for keeping your axolotl's water temperature just right, it can be a bit pricey. But don't worry! There are other clever and wallet-friendly ways to keep things chill. Here are some top tips:

- **Frozen Water Bottles:** Fill some water bottles and pop them in the freezer. When they're frozen solid, you can put them in the tank. They'll slowly melt, releasing cool water and helping to drop the temperature. Keep an eye on the temperature, and swap the bottles as they melt.

- **Tank Fans:** You can get special fans for aquariums that are designed to cool the water. They clip onto the side of the tank and move air over the water, which helps it to cool down.

- **Cool Towels and Ice Packs:** Dampen a towel with cold water and wrap it around the outside of the tank. As the water in the towel evaporates, it'll help to cool the air around the tank, which can help lower the water temperature. Or, you could pop a sealed ice pack or bag of ice on top of the tank (just make sure it's sealed so no water gets in the tank).

- **Air Conditioning:** If your axolotl's tank is in an air-conditioned room, keeping the room nice and cool can help keep the tank cool too.

- **Cooling Fans or Air Coolers:** Point a small fan or air cooler at the tank to blow a chilly breeze over the water, which can help cool it down. Make sure it's not too chilly for your axolotls though!

- **Partial Water Changes with Cooler Water:** Changing some of the water in the tank for water that's a bit cooler can help bring down the overall temperature of the tank.

- **Shady Spots:** Keep the tank out of direct sunlight, as this can make the water too hot. Try to put it somewhere shady, or use curtains or blinds to block the sun.

- **Lighting:** Try to use the tank lights less, or switch to low-intensity LED lights. Too much light can make the tank heat up.

- **Bubble-Driven Filter:** Choose a filter that's powered by bubbles, as these tend to give off less heat than other types. Look for a filter with a lower wattage, as higher wattage means more heat.

- **More Evaporation:** Using a screen top instead of a solid hood can help the water evaporate, which can lower the temperature by 2°F (1°C) or more. You can also add a small airstone or a filter that splashes water across the surface to help this along.

So, there you have it! While a chiller is the best way to control the temperature of your axolotl's tank, there are plenty of other ways to keep things cool if a chiller is out of reach right now. Just remember, always keep a close eye on the temperature and adjust as needed to keep your axolotls happy and healthy.

Water quality

Keeping the water sparkling clean is a top job when caring for your axolotl pals. Dirty or low-quality water can be a real bummer, leading to stress and health issues for your little underwater buddies. Remember, axolotls are water-dwellers; they need clean, bubbly water to thrive.
Imagine you're a water wizard. Your first spell? The Nitrogen Cycle! This magic trick is about calling on some friendly bacteria to transform the icky ammonia that comes from axolotl waste into a less scary thing called nitrite, and then

into an even friendlier thing called nitrate. Let's see together how to do it:

Fill the tank: fill up the tank with water, but remember, it should be dechlorinated - think of it like removing the chlorine from your swimming pool so it's easier on your eyes.

Starting the Nitrogen Cycle: Just like how our stories begin with "Once upon a time...", the nitrogen cycle starts with ammonia. Now, in a brand new tank, there won't be any ammonia, which is typically created by the leftover bits of fish food or the waste they leave behind. To kickstart the cycle, you can drop in a bit of fish food or use a special ammonia source made just for aquariums.

Become a Water Detective: Play detective by using an aquarium water test kit to check the levels of ammonia, nitrites, and nitrates. At first, you'll see that the ammonia levels are going up. But don't worry! With time, the good bacteria (the superheroes of our story) will start to grow and change the ammonia into nitrites. But remember, nitrites, just like villains, can be harmful to our axolotl friends.

Watching Nitrites Rise: As our superhero bacteria get stronger, they'll start changing the villainous ammonia into nitrites. This is when you'll see the ammonia levels start to drop, and the nitrite levels go up. It's like watching the villain lose power and the superheroes gain the upper hand.

Nitrates Join the Story: After a while, another kind of bacteria (let's call them the sidekicks) will join the party. They'll start changing the nitrites into nitrates. While nitrates are kinder to axolotls, we still need to make sure they don't get out of control. So, when you see nitrite levels falling and nitrate levels rising, give yourself a pat on the back - you're almost done with the cycle!

Completing the Cycle: It's like reaching the end of a chapter when you can detect zero ammonia, zero nitrites, and only a bit of nitrates in the tank. This whole journey could take anywhere between 2 to 6 weeks.

But the wizardry doesn't stop there! You also need to perform a water-changing spell from time to time to banish extra nitrates, leftover junk, and other bad stuff from the tank. The size of your tank and the number of axolotl buddies you have will tell you how often you need to perform this spell. Usually, replacing 20% of the water every week or every other week does the trick.

It's also crucial to be a water detective! Use a trustworthy water test kit to keep an eye on pH, ammonia, nitrite, and nitrate levels in the tank. If these levels are out of whack, you need to fix them pronto.

Remember, crummy water quality can lead to a host of troubles for your axolotl buddies, like icky bacterial and fungal infections, fin rot, and more. You can tell the water quality isn't great if it looks cloudy, if there's a lot of algae, if it smells weird, or if your axolotls seem tired or stressed out. And don't forget, besides swapping out the water and keeping tabs on its quality, other ways to keep the water clean include not overfeeding your axolotls, getting rid of any food they haven't eaten right away, and keeping the tank clear of junk and too much algae.

Remember, a happy axolotl is a clean axolotl! So, keep those tanks tidy and your axolotl pals will be thanking you with their happy, smiley faces!

Let's find out together what we should do if the water values do not meet the right parameters:

- **PH, GH, and KH:** These should ideally be at certain levels: PH at 7, GH between 7 and 14, and KH between 3 and 8. Think of them as the comfort zone for your axolotl. If they get too high, you can make your axolotl more comfortable by adding some Indian almond leaves or clean driftwood to the aquarium. But, if they get too low, try using an airstone or adding some shells, coral, or limestone that are bigger than your axolotl's head!

- **Ammonia & Nitrite:** Ideally, these should be at zero — that's what your axolotl likes best! If these levels rise too high, it's like your axolotl's home is getting messy. To clean it up, check for any leftover food or waste and clean it out, or you could add some live plants. But if these levels get too low, you can add a magic potion called FLUVAL Cycle, some liquid ammonia, or even some axolotl food or waste to your aquarium. This is only needed if you're just setting up your aquarium.

- **Nitrate:** Your axolotl likes it when this is between 5 and 20. If it gets too high, it's like your axolotl's water is getting stale, so you'll need to replace some of the water with fresh water treated with a special conditioner called Seachum Prime. If it's between 20-40ppm, change a quarter of the water; if it's between 40-80ppm, change half of the water; and if it's between 80-160ppm, change three-quarters of the water. If the nitrate level gets too low, you can wait to see if the ammonia and nitrites rise or you can add FLUVAL Cycle, liquid ammonia, food or waste to boost the cycling process. Remember, this is only needed if you're just setting up your aquarium

Substrate

One golden rule to remember when picking the perfect ground covering, or substrate, for your axolotl pals is to say "No!" to pebbles, tiny stones, and gravel. Why, you might ask? Well, axolotls have a quirky way of eating. They like to slurp up their food, and if there's a pebble nearby, they might swallow that too! Imagine trying to digest a rock — ouch! Not only could this cause a nasty blockage in their tummy, but it might also put our axolotl friends in serious danger.

What should we use instead, then? Sand is the superstar choice for axolotls! It's too fine to cause any blockages and even if they swallow some by accident, axolotls can easily spit it back out. Plus, adding some live plants and a cover or slits over the sand can really spruce up your tank and make it easier to see your little water buddies.

Now, not all sand is created equal. Sand comes in all sorts of shapes and sizes, so you want to make sure you're picking the right one. Avoid sand that's too big or sharp - it can have tiny splinters. Ideally, the sand should be smaller than 1 mm. When you're setting up your sand beach, don't pile it up more than 1-2 inches high. Give it a good stir with a rod now and then to stop gas and aerobic bacteria from building up. And remember to wash it thoroughly before you put it in the tank, and check regularly to make sure the water is flowing nicely.

Ceramic tiles can also be a pretty cool option. They come in lots of fun colors and are easy to clean. But, watch out for the shiny glazed ones! These tiles can have metal salts in them that could leak into the water over time. So, make sure to go for unglazed tiles. If you decide to add some plants to a tank with a bare bottom, you'll need to put them in pots.
Slate tiles are another groovy choice. All you need to do is tell the store the size of your tank base, and they'll give you the perfect sized slate tiles!

Some axolotl parents might think about using big river stones, ones that are larger than an axolotl's head. It might look cool, but remember, these rocks can make it tough to clean the tank. Food could sneak under the stones, making it hard for your axolotl to reach and making the tank a nightmare to clean compared to other options. So, always think carefully before you choose your substrate!

Tank Decor, Hides and Plants

Think of setting up your axolotl tank like creating a cozy home for your water-dwelling friend. In this underwater castle, you add hideouts and maybe some plants—real or pretend—to make your axolotl feel safe and secure. Not only does it make your axolotl super happy, but it also transforms your tank into a little underwater paradise that's pleasing to your eyes too!

But hang on! Before you dive in and start adding everything you can think of, remember to do your homework. We need to make sure we're only adding things that are safe for our axolotl pals. That random rock you found in the garden? It might seem like a good idea, but it could have harmful substances on it that could hurt your axolotl. And seashells might look pretty, but they can actually make the water too alkaline for our little buddies. So, let's leave those out.

Axolotl Hides

Axolotls are like little vampires—they're not big fans of the light! That's why it's super important to create lots of hiding places in their tank. These hideouts give them a place to escape the light and have some chill-out time. You should aim to have at least 1 or 2 hideouts for each adult axolotl. This ensures they have plenty of space to play and relax. If you're feeling crafty, you can even make your own hideouts! Some pet owners like to use PVC pipes for this, but you need to make sure they don't have any sharp edges. A quick sanding should do the trick, as axolotls have delicate skin that can easily get cut.

Of course, you can also find hideouts in pet stores. Just remember to double-check for any sharp edges to keep your axolotl safe. You'll find all sorts of fun designs to choose from!

Axolotl Tank Plants

Axolotls love to play in the water and they're not picky about whether the plants in their tank are real or fake. They're just excited to explore the new additions to their tank!

If you decide to go for real plants, there's an added bonus— they help create a healthier environment in the tank. Real plants take part in the nitrogen cycle, producing oxygen and absorbing nitrates from the water. But no matter what you decide, your axolotl will be thrilled with their underwater garden!

Tank Cleaning

Keeping your axolotl's tank sparkling clean is a bit like caring for a tiny aquatic garden. A good rule of thumb is to change out about 20-25% of the tank water each week. But before you fill 'er up, make sure to treat the fresh water with a water conditioner to get rid of any chlorine or chloramines. You see, these chemicals are not axolotl-friendly and can mess up the nitrogen cycle, which keeps the tank environment healthy for your water buddy.

But remember, don't empty the tank completely or give it a big scrub down. Instead, think about investing in a good gravel vacuum. This handy gadget makes it a breeze to clean and remove waste and leftovers, saving you time and effort.

Another cool tool to consider is a turkey baster. Yes, you heard that right! You might think it's just for Thanksgiving, but it's actually great for spot cleaning your tank. It's like a little underwater vacuum, slurping up bits of leftover food or waste from the tank floor. Bonus: you can even use it to feed your axolotl!

Now, when it comes to cleaning the filters and other tank equipment, always use the tank water. Tap water can mess with the nitrogen cycle, which we definitely don't want. Plus, it helps to avoid introducing any chlorine or chloramines into the tank. Be extra careful when cleaning the filters, as they are the high-rise apartments for the beneficial bacteria that help keep your tank in balance.

UNDERSTANDING YOUR AXOLOTL'S MENU

Axolotls might be endangered in the wild, but they're loved as pets in many homes. If you're going to invite an axolotl into your family, you'll need to understand what it likes to eat and how to look after it. Axolotls are carnivores, meaning they love to munch on meaty treats, but that doesn't mean they only want steak for dinner! They enjoy a variety of food, just like us. High-protein meals are their absolute favorite.

Axolotls have tiny teeth that are excellent at grabbing onto food. But, you won't see them chewing away like we do because they suck in their food and gulp it down whole. This way of eating is called suction feeding. Whether the meal is alive or not doesn't really bother them, but baby axolotls prefer their dinner to do a little dance before they eat it. The movement gets their attention and encourages them to eat.

When it comes to feeding axolotls, you might notice they're a bit messy. They tend to leave a lot of leftovers at the bottom of their tank, but hey, we all know someone who's a bit messy when they eat, right?

How Often Should You Feed Your Axolotl?

From tiny hatchlings to full-grown adults, axolotls need different types of meals and feeding frequencies. Just like you don't eat the same food or the same amount as you did when you were a baby, your axolotl's feeding needs will change as they grow. Let's embark on this tasty journey to discover how we can best meet our little water buddy's appetite at each stage of their life!

First things first, let's talk about the 'itty-bitty' hatchlings, those under an inch. You're going to have to feed them thrice a day - yep, you heard it right! In their first month, they'll munch on exciting live foods like little baby brine shrimp, micro-worms tinier than you can imagine, the odd-looking vinegar eels, and the whitest worms of all!

Next comes the 'not-so-tiny' babies, between 1 and 3 inches. Now, you only need to feed them twice a day. Continue with the live food but introduce them to slightly bigger buddies like the blackworms, daphnia, adult brine shrimp, and something juicy like bloodworms.

As they grow up and become teenagers (we call them 'juveniles' and they're 3-9 inches), keep the feeding times at twice a day. Now's the time to bring in some gourmet food to their table. Introduce pellets (1-2 per inch), earthworms (but remember, smaller than your axolotl's head), something squiggly like reg wigglers (make sure they're blanched and cooled), repashy pie, and the bloodworms and krill as a little treat!

Now, when your axolotl has fully grown into an adult (over 9 inches), you'll have to feed them just thrice a week. Their diet will consist of pellets, earthworms (you can feed them half or a whole), reg wigglers, repashy pie, and occasional treats. For treats, they can have bloodworms, krill, raw frozen salmon, raw frozen shrimp, and live shrimp or fish.

You'll soon figure out how much your axolotl wants to eat because if they've had enough, they'll simply stop eating. Looking at your axolotl can also give you some clues about how much to feed them. If their body is about as wide as their head, you're doing a good job.

Tips for a Fun and Safe Axolotl Feeding Time

Feeding axolotls can be a fun activity for the whole family! Here are a few tips to make meal times easier:

- Long tweezers can be a great tool for feeding your axolotl, especially when you're using live food. It keeps things neat and tidy. Just make sure the tweezers don't have sharp edges that could hurt your little water buddy.

- After each meal, it's important to clean up any leftovers in the tank to keep the water fresh and safe. If food is left to rot, it can spoil the water and make your axolotl unwell. Allow about 20 minutes for your axolotl to finish its meal after which you remove the leftover food.

- A turkey baster isn't just for Thanksgiving anymore! Use it to deliver food directly into the tank, move food around, or even clean up uneaten bits. It's a great tool for keeping your axolotl's home neat and tidy.

- Baby axolotls love live food. The movement of their dinner helps them find it, so make sure to provide a wiggle or two during feeding time.

- Axolotls are night owls, just like owls! They're most active after the sun goes down, so try to feed them more in the evening. So, lights out, dinner's up! It's time for your axolotl's nighttime feast.

Your Axolotl's Meal Plan

Just like in the wild, axolotls need their meals to be as close as possible to what they'd naturally find in lakes and rivers. So, to make them feel right at home, let's explore the menu they would choose if they could shop for themselves!

Raw, fresh meals are always the best choice for your axolotl, as these are most like what they would eat in the wild. But, if you can't find fresh food, there are frozen options that your axolotl will happily gobble up. While frozen food might not be as nutritious as fresh food, it's safer because it doesn't carry any harmful bugs or parasites.

Here are a few food options for your axolotl:

- **Nightcrawlers/Earthworms:** These squiggly snacks are a favorite for axolotls. They're nutritious and can be found easily. Remember to clean them properly before feeding them to your axolotl, and make sure they're cut into bite-size pieces.

- **Brine Shrimp:** Baby axolotls love brine shrimp. They're a good source of nutrition and help with the bone development of your little water buddy. But remember, brine shrimp don't live long in the tank. So feed your axolotl fresh shrimp and clean up any leftovers promptly to avoid any changes to the water's quality.

- **Daphnia:** Daphnia is another good option for young axolotls. They're small, nutritious, and a great source of food for the little ones. However, be careful where you buy them from as they can carry parasites.

- **Tilapia:** This fish is a good option, but make sure to choose freshwater tilapia over saltwater ones. Too much salt and minerals can be harmful to axolotls.

- **Beef Heart:** A bit on the fatty side, beef hearts are best used as occasional treats.

- **Maggots:** These insect larvae can help your axolotl put on some weight, especially when they're recovering from an illness.

- **Mealworms:** Treat your axolotl to mealworms every once in a while. But be careful as their hard shells can cause issues in your axolotl's tummy.

- **Pellet Food:** This ready-to-eat food is great because it provides all the nutrients your axolotl needs. Look for sinking, soft pellets like Hikari Massivore Delite, Tetra Reptomin Floating Sticks, and Tetra Reptomin Plus Floating Sticks.

- **Frozen Food:** If you can't get hold of live food, frozen options like bloodworms and brine shrimp are a great choice. They're safe and easy to store, though they can get a bit messy than pellet feed once defrosted.

Mixing Up Mealtime

Just like us humans, axolotls enjoy a smorgasbord of food choices. Giving them a yummy mix of different things to nibble on ensures they get all the nutrients they need. Plus, it keeps mealtimes fun and interesting - imagine having to eat the same thing every day, yawn!

In their natural homes, axolotls munch on a mini buffet of small creatures. Tiny insects, little fish, crunchy crustaceans, and wriggly worms are all part of their menu. As a caring axolotl guardian, you can bring this delicious diversity into your axolotl's tank. One day, you could serve a plate of earthworms. The next, maybe a shrimp cocktail of brine shrimp. And for a little change, how about some specially made axolotl pellets every so often?

Just remember, different foods come with different benefits. Take earthworms, for example. They're like the axolotl's version of a protein shake, but they don't have much fat. That makes them a perfect regular meal for your water buddy. Then there's brine shrimp and daphnia — they're full of good stuff like essential fats and vitamins. And don't forget the pellets; they're kind of like the axolotl's daily multivitamin, packed with necessary vitamins and minerals.

Just like kids need different food from grown-ups, little axolotls have different dietary needs from the grown-up ones. Baby axolotls, growing super fast, need lots of protein-rich food. Adult axolotls, on the other hand, need a balanced diet of protein, fats, and fiber.

But watch out! Not everything is safe for your axolotl to eat. Foods with hard shells or sharp bones could be dangerous, and large meals could be hard for them to handle. As a simple guide, make sure their food is no bigger than their head.

Lastly, while mixing up your axolotl's meals is great, don't forget to keep an eye on their reactions. Every axolotl is unique, and some may have favorite foods or even food they don't tolerate well. And always remember, clean up any leftovers quickly to keep their tank sparkling clean and safe.

KEEPING YOUR AXOLOTL CLEAN AND HEALTHY

Common health issues and how to prevent and address them

Whoa! Did you know that even in the most awesome underwater castle, your axolotl buddy might feel a bit down sometimes? They can get sick just like we do, with things like tummy aches and icky fungus! But don't worry! We're here to teach you how to make them feel better. Sometimes, the troublemaker is the water they live in - not changing it often enough, not keeping it clean, or having some uninvited guests like bad bacteria can make your water buddy feel yucky.

"Stress Signs? What's that?" you may ask. Here are some things to look out for:

1. **Curly Gills:** Picture your axolotl giving a big grin, with gills curling towards the front of their face. That's not a smile, it's a sign of unhappy water! Run a water test and if needed, do a water change. If the gills keep looking like curly fries even with good water, then it's time to call a specialist.

2. **Vanishing Gills:** If your axolotl's gills are looking a little thin, the water could be too "ammonia-y" or full of other nasty stuff. This usually happens when we forget to clean the aquarium or the water's nitrogen cycle is off. Just remember: No bad chemicals and keep the water clean! Doing a mini (20%) water change every week can help keep the ammonia, nitrate, and nitrite levels low. And if after doing all that, things don't improve, it may be time for a filter check-up!

3. **Curling Tail Tip:** A curly tail might look cute on a pig, but on an axolotl? It might be a red flag for stress or sickness. Double-check the water conditions and if everything seems okay, your little buddy might be sick. In that case, talk to a specialist or reach out to the Axolotl Planet team right away.

4. **Not Hungry:** It's not normal for your axolotl to turn down its favorite meal. Too hot water or dirty water can steal their appetite away. Check the water temperature and cleanliness. Other things like bullying tank mates or some sneaky bad germs can also make them lose their appetite. Keep a close eye on their surroundings!

5. **Big Gulps of Air:** Your axolotl can breathe in water and air, which is pretty cool! But if it's frequently going up for air, it could be because the water is too warm. Make sure to keep it between 65–70°F, but never above 72°F.

6. **Floating or Upside Down Floating:** Axolotls love to float around, but if you see your buddy floating upside down, it might mean that they've swallowed some air and can't balance themselves. This could be serious, so get in touch with a specialist or the Axolotl Planet team right away.

7. **Being Super Quiet:** If your usually playful axolotl starts ignoring you, it might be because they're stressed. Watch out for signs like not wanting to eat or interact.

8. **Going Pale:** Axolotls can change their color a little bit depending on their surroundings. But if your buddy

looks really pale, it might be stressed, hurt or worse. Reach out to a specialist if you see any sudden changes in their color.

Always remember, our axolotl friends need our love and care just like any other pet. By keeping an eye on these signs, you can make sure they stay happy and healthy in their underwater kingdom!

Common Diseases

Sickly New Tank

Imagine if your tank is a small, water world. It needs time to grow the right tiny creatures that keep it clean. Sometimes, though, it doesn't have enough time to grow these good bacteria, and harmful chemicals like ammonia or nitrite might build up. This could happen for various reasons like too much feeding or too many axolotls. But don't worry, with frequent water changes, adding good bacteria, and figuring out the problem, this can be sorted out!

Worn-Out Old Tank

Sometimes, an older tank might have too much nitrate. This can make your axolotl feel unwell and show things like bulging eyes. Frequent water changes and fixing the problem at its root can make your axolotl's home healthy again!

Too Hot to Handle

Axolotls prefer cool water. If the water gets warmer than 72°F, your axolotl may stop eating, become bloated, or keep floating around. Remember, it's good to have a tank cooler to avoid this problem.

Gravel Trouble

Gravels can seem like a tasty snack to axolotls, especially when they're really hungry! If your axolotl eats some by accident, it might be able to throw them up, but sometimes we need to help them get it out safely. Remember, it's better to avoid gravel in your axolotl's home.

Bacteria Bad Guys

Some bacteria, like Aeromonas and Pseudomonas, can make your axolotl sick. They might stop eating, and in worse situations, they may look bloated. If this happens, you should talk to a vet who can prescribe some medicine. Keeping the tank cooler and changing the water often can help your axolotl get better.

Funky Fungus

Sometimes, axolotls can get sick with something called Mycobacteriosis, which is pretty similar to the bacteria bad guys.Stress, ubiquitous microorganisms, and exposure to live foods can predispose axolotls to this condition. If your axolotl gets this, a vet can check and confirm it.

Pesty Parasites

If you feed your axolotl live fish, they might bring along unwanted guests like parasites. These can be treated with special medication.

Skin Scrapes

Axolotls have soft skin that can get hurt easily. When it's the time of year for them to find a partner, they might get into some fights. If this happens, the injuries need to be treated so they don't get infected. Sometimes, a bit of their limb might need to be removed, but don't worry - axolotls can regrow their limbs!

Strange White Fluff

Sometimes, a fluffy white growth called Saprolegnia can show up on your axolotl's skin. This can happen if the water isn't clean or if your axolotl gets into a fight. The fluff needs to be treated, and if it's on a limb, that part might need to be removed and treated just like a scrape.

Neoplasia

Axolotls can develop benign tumors, typically involving the pigment cells. Removal is not necessary unless they cause obstruction or are at risk of traumatic injury.

Toxic Trouble

Some things that we use to clean tanks can make axolotls sick, such as malachite green, copper-based treatments, and tetracycline, are unsafe for axolotls and should be avoided. Excessive salt treatment can also cause harm. There are other things that are safe to use though, like certain antiseptics and antibiotics.

Funky Fungal Infections

"Fungal infection" is a big word for something called Mycosis. This can happen if the tank isn't kept clean or if something new brings in the fungus. Using water from another axolotl owner and special leaves during water changes can help. It's best not to use chemicals at first and change the water often instead.

This guide is your friend in your journey to understand and care for your axolotl. But remember, it's not a replacement for a professional vet's advice. Axolotls are unique little creatures, each with their own special needs. When your axolotl feels under the weather, or you spot something fishy, don't delay and reach out to your vet at once. Even with the info in this guide, sometimes, things aren't as simple as they seem.

Remember, being proactive and having a good vet are two keys to your axolotl's health and happiness. Building trust with a vet who knows about axolotls can be a lifesaver! If you're ever unsure, always ask your vet. It's the best gift you can give to your axolotl.

Importance of Quarantine and Sterilization

Axolotls can catch illnesses from new tank buddies, food, or even new decorations. To keep them safe:

- Quarantine: If you're bringing a new friend or item into your axolotl's world, keep them separate for two to four weeks. Watch them closely for any signs they might not be feeling well. The quarantine space should be just like your axolotl's main tank.

- Sterilize: Clean everything you use for your axolotl like nets or feeders with a solution of water and a little bleach (10% bleach). Rinse them well with clean water and let them dry before using them with your axolotl.

Taking these steps will help keep your axolotl healthy. They are a big part of being an axolotl owner.

Signs of a Healthy Axolotl

Knowing what a healthy axolotl looks like is just as important as knowing when they're sick. Here are some signs your axolotl is doing great:

- **Always Hungry:** A healthy axolotl loves to eat. They'll be excited to see food and will gobble it up without a second thought.

- **Curious Creatures:** While they're not the busiest of pets, healthy axolotls do like to look around their tank, especially during mealtime.

- **Smooth Skin and Puffy Gills:** Look out for smooth skin and full, feathery gills that usually stand up.

- **Sparkling Eyes:** Healthy axolotls have clear, bright eyes.

- **Regular Bathroom Breaks:** Regular bathroom breaks are a sign that everything's going well inside.

- **Just Right Weight:** Healthy axolotls don't gain or lose weight suddenly.

- **Balanced Swimmers:** Healthy axolotls can control their movements and position in the water easily.

The more you observe your axolotl, the better you'll know them. If you ever think something's off, don't hesitate to contact a vet who knows about axolotls.

Just a note - while these signs generally indicate a healthy axolotl, each axolotl is unique and may behave or look slightly different. If you're worried about your axolotl's health, don't hesitate to talk to your vet.

AXOLOTL SOCIAL LIFE AND PLAYTIME

Axolotls are the solo adventurers of the animal kingdom, they love their alone time and aren't the type to make buddies with others. Imagine them as the superheroes of their own underwater world, not needing a sidekick. They like to live in their own special corner, away from other axolotls.

You know what's super interesting about grown-up axolotls? They can share a tank, especially if it's a boy and a girl axolotl. And guess what? They can have little axolotl babies. Pretty cool, right? You can tell a boy from a girl axolotl by the shape of their cloaca, which is a special opening under their tail. Boys have a bumpy cloaca, while girls have a flat one.

But remember, axolotls like to be the lone rangers of their tank. So if you have other aquarium pets, they might not get along. They don't really like to share their space and can sometimes nip at each other. So if you have more than one axolotl, it's best to get a bigger tank to keep everyone happy.

Young axolotls, well, they're a little more feisty. They sometimes like to munch on their smaller buddies, yikes! So, if you want to keep a bunch of axolotls together, make sure they're about the same size to prevent any munching mishaps. Adult axolotls are much nicer to their friends and don't usually bother each other. But if things get too crowded, they can start behaving a bit like their younger selves. It's best to always keep an eye on them.

Ideas for toys and activities

Axolotls may not like toys or play dates, but they still know how to have fun. They like to spend their time hanging out at the bottom of the tank, playing hide-and-seek in plants or other hiding spots.

Even without toys, axolotls know how to enjoy themselves. They can put on a dinner show, snapping at their food and tossing it around. They also love to explore, digging in the tank's bottom, darting about in quick bursts, or even following your finger on the glass. Sometimes, they can be quite the performers, rising to the top of the tank to gulp air and blow bubbles, or just floating around. If they share their tank, they might even start a game of tag!

These creatures are nothing like our everyday pets, like dogs or cats. They're a little more reserved when it comes to physical contact. Yet, that doesn't mean you can't form a bond with them. Start by carefully placing your hand in the water, and let them decide to come closer. As they grow comfortable, you may have the chance to lightly caress their tail or belly. Just remember, always approach with respect and consideration for their space. With a little bit of patience and care, your axolotl might just evolve into your new best friend.

To make their tank more appealing, consider these fun additions:

- ## Hiding Places

Axolotls have a knack for a good game of hide-and-seek. To fuel this passion, consider adding some intriguing hiding spots. These could range from PVC pipes and clay pots to rock caves or even store-bought aquarium hides. Just remember to make sure that these hideouts are safe — devoid of sharp edges or harmful chemicals, and spacious enough to ensure your axolotl won't get stuck. If you keep these pointers in mind, you can craft the perfect secret sanctuary for your aquatic companion.

- ## Airstone

While axolotls typically enjoy peaceful waters, a touch of liveliness with an airstone can be an exciting change for them. It's truly a sight to behold when they swim towards the airstone and let the bubbles carry them to the surface. Besides, the additional oxygen it provides can help maintain their gill health, keeping them vibrant and active.

- ## Reptile Hammock

Ever heard of a hammock for your pet? A mesh reptile hammock creates an extra lounging spot halfway up the tank. Axolotls can either chill on top or have fun hiding underneath. These hammocks are pocket-friendly and can make your axolotl's tank feel like a vacation spot.

- ## Silk or Live Plants

Plants aren't just for decoration. They're great for providing hiding spots and places to rest. Go for silk or live plants to avoid any sharp edges that could hurt your axolotl. You can choose from different colors and designs to create a tank that's as unique as your axolotl.

- ## Moss Balls

Axolotls love to push around moss balls. They're a type of algae that's super easy to care for, and they help keep the water clean. Just make sure the moss balls are bigger than your axolotl's head to prevent any snack-time accidents.

- Driftwood and Large Rocks

Natural elements like driftwood and rocks make a great playground for axolotls. They love to climb over rocks and hide behind driftwood. Just watch out for any sharp edges or small rocks that could be a choking hazard. Larger slates are safe and also add a nice touch to the tank.

Remember, the most important thing is to ensure your axolotl's space is safe and enjoyable. With these toys and accessories, your axolotl will have the coolest home in the neighborhood!

AXOLOTL GROWTH AND LIFESPAN

The different stages of an Axolotl's life

Axolotls are quite the fascinating creatures, don't you think? These aquatic buddies don't go through a typical metamorphosis like other amphibians. In fact, because of a cool trait called neoteny, axolotls get to keep their youthful looks all the way to adulthood! Unlike most amphibians that start off in water and then transition to living on land, axolotls are water-lovers all their lives, just like some types of salamanders. Now, isn't that unique?

Want to know more? Great! The axolotl life story unfolds in three main acts: the egg, the larva, and the adult stage. In this exciting journey, we'll also take a look at some smaller scenes that occur within each act. Ready? Let's dive in!

Stage 1 - The Amazing Axolotl Egg

Like many stories, the axolotl tale begins with an egg - a fertilized egg to be precise. The mother axolotl usually lays a lot of eggs - think about 1000 in a season! Now, these fertilized eggs are pretty special because they contain everything needed to make a brand-new baby axolotl.

The Single-Cell Embryo

In the very beginning, each egg is home to a single-celled embryo. This little one is an axolotl-to-be, but it's still a work in progress. Protected by a jelly-like coating, it's about 0,08 inches in diameter - that's really tiny!

The Multicellular Clump

Then something exciting happens. The single cell starts to multiply, forming a clump of cells within the egg. These cells begin to shape up, taking on features like the body and the head that make them look like mini-axolotl larvae. And when they're about 0,4 inches big, they're ready for the next big adventure - hatching!

Stage 2 - The Adventurous Axolotl Larva

After about two weeks of growing inside the egg, the baby axolotl, now called a larva, is ready to say hello to the world. The larva stage also has some cool sub-stages, which depend on whether the axolotl has limbs yet.

The Limbless Larva

In the first part of this act, the axolotl larva doesn't have any legs - it looks like a tiny fish with a long tail and a thin, see-through skin. In this stage, you can actually spot the beginnings of gill buds, which will grow into the lovely feathery gills axolotls are known for.

Larva With Front Limbs

In about a week or so, the larva starts to grow its two front legs, each with four toes! And during this time, those gill buds keep developing into beautiful, feathery gills. By the time it's 15 days old, the axolotl is about 1 inches long, with fully-grown front legs and the buds of its hind legs starting to show.

Larva With Front & Back Limbs

As our little axolotl grows over the next few weeks, it will have grown all four of its legs - two front feet each with four toes, and two back feet each with five toes. By this time, our little one is no longer a larva but a juvenile axolotl, about 4 cm long and with all the physical features of an adult axolotl, save for size, weight, and breeding capacity. But don't worry.

Stage 3 - Adult Axolotl

Once an axolotl grows up and is ready to start a family, we say they have become adults. They've reached a milestone that we call 'maturity'. Just like in many animal kingdom stories, the males and females find each other in their unique, traditional way to have babies. After the female axolotl lays her eggs, she's ready to begin the cycle all over again, preparing for the next bunch of baby axolotls.

You know, it can take somewhere from six months to a whole year for an axolotl to grow into an adult! Some may even take their sweet time and reach maturity after 18 to 24 months. These intriguing water buddies can be part of your family for quite a long time, as their average lifespan falls between 12 to 15 years. Just remember, how long they live and how happy they are really depends on how well we take care of them!

Life Cycle Stage	Duration	Size(inch/mm)
Fertilized Egg -Embryo	After laying	1/16 inch 2 mm
Fertilized Egg -Clump of Cells	15 Days	1/16 inch – 3/8 inch 2 mm – 10 mm
Larva -Limbless	15 Days	3/8 inch – 1 inch 10 mm – 2.5 cm
Larva -Front Legs Only	15 Days	1 inch – 1 1/2 inches 2.5 cm – 4 cm
Larva (Juvenile) -Both Legs	4.5 Months (At least)	1 1/2 inches – 8 inches 4 cm – 25 cm

Adult	5 to 15 years (in their wild). 10 to 20 years (in their captive).	8 inches – 10 inches 25 cm – 30 cm (When fully grown)

Monitoring Growth

Keeping an eye on your axolotl's size isn't only about checking if they're getting bigger, it's about making sure they're growing healthy and happy. If there are any hiccups along the way, you'll want to spot them as soon as possible! Here's a deeper dive into how you can keep track of your axolotl's growth:

Regular Measurement

You might remember, axolotls usually grow to their full size within 1.5 to 2 years. They tend to grow the most during their first birthday year. It's quite common for an axolotl to grow about 1 to 2 inches per month during this time, but this can change based on things like their unique DNA and the environment they live in.

Measuring your axolotl is easy peasy! Just grab a smooth, waterproof ruler or tape measure. Put it in the tank right next to your axolotl. Then, without picking them up, gently encourage your axolotl to line up next to the ruler.

Remember, we measure axolotls from the tip of their nose to where their tail starts, but we don't include the tail in the measurement.

Keep an eye on the inches (or centimeters) and you should notice a slow and steady increase over time. But, if your axolotl stays the same size for a few months, it might mean they're not growing as they should be. There could be a few reasons for this, like not enough good food, water that isn't clean, or some other health problems.

Don't forget, axolotls don't always grow at the same speed. As they start to become grown-ups, they tend to slow down a bit, and they might even stop growing once they've reached their full size. Plus, just like people, some axolotls are naturally bigger or smaller than others because of the way their genes are.

Remember, every axolotl is unique and can be different. If you're ever worried about your axolotl's size, it's always a good idea to talk to a vet or someone who knows a lot about axolotls. They can give you advice that's specially made for your axolotl's needs.

Observing Physical Changes

Your axolotl is going to change in more ways than just getting bigger. Male axolotls usually have a slimmer body and a wider tail, while females tend to be a bit chunkier with shorter, plumper tails. The opening called the cloaca, which axolotls use to get rid of waste, is different in boys and girls too - boys have a puffy cloaca, and girls have one that's smaller and less noticeable. If you notice any sudden or big changes in your axolotl's body, it might mean something's wrong, and you should get it checked out.

Monitoring Appetite

How much your axolotl wants to eat can tell you a lot about how they're feeling. Axolotls usually love to chow down, but if their diet or eating habits change, it might affect how they grow. Make sure they're getting food that's right for how old they are, and keep an eye out for any changes in how they eat. If your axolotl suddenly doesn't want to eat or wants to eat a lot more, it could be a sign they're not feeling well. If you notice any big changes, it's time to take a trip to the vet.

Keeping a Growth Journal

Writing down what you notice in a size diary can help you keep track of what's normal for your axolotl and how they're growing. It's also a great thing to bring when you go to the vet. You should write down not just how long they are, but also what they're doing, changes in how they eat, color changes, how often they shed, and anything else that seems different. This way, you can spot any small changes that you might not notice otherwise, but could mean there's a problem.

Consultation with Experts

While it's a great idea for you to keep track of your axolotl's size, it's also super helpful to have someone who knows a lot about axolotls to check on them. Regular visits to a vet who knows axolotls well can help you make sure your pet is growing and changing in the right way. They can also tell you more about the best food and living space for your axolotl based on how old they are and what they need. If your axolotl suddenly gets bigger or smaller, or starts acting or looking different, talk to an expert right away. By keeping a close eye on how your axolotl is growing and knowing what to look for, you're doing your part to make sure your water friend is healthy and happy.

By monitoring your Axolotl's growth closely and understanding what to look for, you're taking an active role in ensuring the health and happiness of your aquatic friend.

RESPONSIBLE
PET OWNERSHIP

Is an Axolotl Right for You?

We all dream of having a pet to call our own when we're kids. We swear up and down that we'll take care of it and provide everything it needs. But as time goes on, we realize taking care of a pet isn't as simple as it seemed. It's not just about giving them a safe and happy home. It also means thinking about our own lives and whether we can really give what the pet needs.

So, if you're thinking about making an axolotl your new best buddy, there are a few big things to think about: your daily routine, how much money you can spend, your lifestyle, safety, and any health issues you might have.

Budget

Before diving into axolotl ownership, it's important to consider your savings. While these enchanting aquatic creatures might seem like a budget-friendly pet, their care can cost more than you'd expect. Like all pets, axolotls require a particular diet, a comfortable habitat, and occasionally, medical attention. Veterinary expenses can accumulate swiftly if they fall ill.
So, before you commit to bringing an axolotl into your home, be sure you're prepared to handle the financial responsibility. A chat with a vet who specializes in axolotls can provide insights into the expected costs and overall needs of these unique creatures.

Your Daily Routine

Also, ponder on your daily routine. If you're at school most of the day, will you have ample time to care for your axolotl once you're home? If you're home-schooled, will there be enough pause periods in your day to feed and monitor your axolotl? Axolotls aren't high-maintenance, but they still require regular attention.

Life Style

Think about your lifestyle outside of school. What are your hobbies? Do you frequently travel? Ensuring that owning an axolotl fits seamlessly into your life is vital. You'll need to offer consistent care and also ensure there's sufficient space in your home for a new pet.

It wouldn't be fair to the axolotl if you discovered you were too preoccupied or your schedule was incompatible after you brought it home. Thus, it's advisable to consult with a vet or refer to reliable sources about axolotls before making your decision.

Safety

Safety always comes first! Even the most mild-mannered pets, like axolotls, can be somewhat challenging for young children to manage. Ensure that you and your family are prepared to accept the responsibility that comes with having an axolotl in the house.

Research of pet

Finally, prior to purchasing an axolotl, strive to understand them thoroughly. As unique and relatively uncommon pets, even minor mistakes can have significant consequences for these adorable amphibians. Acquaint yourself with their natural habitat and preferred diet. Always remember, a bit of research beforehand can spare you from potential problems in the future.

Tips on Ethical Adoption and Buying Practices

If you're thrilled about the idea of welcoming an axolotl as the newest member of your aquatic family, that's great! We want to ensure we take all the right steps to keep our water-loving friends happy and safe. Here is a helpful guide to follow:

Find the Axolotl Experts: First things first, put on your detective hat and seek out the top-notch axolotl breeders or fans out there. They should adore axolotls just like you and should take good care of these interesting creatures. Make sure the tanks they live in are spotless, and the axolotls appear content, with no signs of illness or injury. If you notice any health issues, or if the breeder doesn't seem knowledgeable about optimal axolotl conditions, it's best to continue your search elsewhere. Remember, asking questions is your secret weapon!

Say No to Wild Axolotls: It's a big no-no to take axolotls from their wild homes. This could hurt their numbers in the wild. Instead, let's stick to axolotls born and bred in a safe, controlled environment. They're better suited to live as pets, and this way, we're helping keep the wild population healthy.

Check Out the Local Scene: If possible, visit your local breeders or pet stores that know a thing or two about amphibians. This gives you a chance to meet the axolotls in person and see where they live. Make sure everything's clean and comfy for them - they deserve a nice home!

Choose a Healthy Buddy: When picking your axolotl, look for one with bright eyes, all its limbs and gills in place, a healthy skin coat, and a strong, energetic body. Any signs of sickness, like skin spots, tiredness, or missing limbs, should be a signal to find a healthier friend.

Consider Being a Hero: Occasionally, axolotls need a savior. If they're in need of a new home or haven't been treated well, you have the chance to rescue or adopt one of these charming beings. You'll not only gain a new friend, but you'll also feel great about helping out!

Be Ready for Your New Friend: Prior to welcoming an axolotl into your home, it's crucial to be well-prepared. These little guys require a specific habitat temperature, clean water, and sufficient space to explore. Be sure to have everything set to make them as content and cozy as possible.

Support Axolotl Protectors: You can also contribute to axolotl welfare by supporting organizations that strive to protect them in their natural habitats. This ensures these unique, always-grinning critters will continue to thrive.

Keep in mind, when we invite an axolotl into our homes, we commit to their well-being. Let's ensure we're doing everything we can to provide them with a safe, joyful, and nurturing environment. By following these guidelines, you're well on your way to becoming a super-duper axolotl guardian!

CONCLUSION

Wow, we've been on such an incredible adventure together, haven't we? Exploring the amazing world of Axolotls, those enchanting water critters with magical abilities like regeneration, and learning about their delicate situation out in the wild.

Together, we've navigated the world of creating the perfect home for an Axolotl. Do you remember how we talked about picking the coziest aquarium and ensuring the water feels just like their natural habitat? And oh, the food! The exploration of the Axolotl's menu and how to keep their tummies happy was quite a journey, wasn't it?

We dove into the nitty-gritty of keeping our Axolotl's house clean and bright, and we discussed some of the health hiccups they might face and how we can help. Remember, a tidy home is a happy home, especially for an Axolotl!

Then, we peeked into their social life - do Axolotls prefer their own company, or do they enjoy having tank pals? And let's not forget the fun part – toys and activities to keep our water buddy bubbling with joy!

We've also travelled through the different stages of an Axolotl's life, from the moment they're a tiny egg to the time they mature into adults. We've shared tips on nurturing them, helping them grow strong and healthy, and ensuring they have a life filled with happiness.

Finally, we emphasized that owning an Axolotl is not just fun and games, but a serious commitment. Remember, being an Axolotl's friend requires lots of love, care, and attention. Continue to learn and share your newfound knowledge about these extraordinary creatures. Who knows, you might inspire someone else to help protect and conserve Axolotls!

We hope you've loved your journey through "Axolotl Care Made Easy" as much as we've loved crafting this guide for you. If you've enjoyed reading this book and think it could be helpful to other Axolotl friends, we would greatly appreciate it if you could share your feedback.

Your opinion matters to us and can help other readers decide whether this book might be right for them. So, if you have a moment, please leave a review or comment. We'd love to hear what you think about the book and if there are any topics you'd like us to delve deeper into in the future.

Thank you once again for stepping into the world of Axolotls with us. We look forward to continuing this journey of discovery with you. Good luck and enjoy your time with your little water wizard!

References

- "A Guide to Keeping Axolotls - by NT Labs." https://www.ntlabs.co.uk/knowledge-hub/a-guide-to-keeping-axolotls/

- "Amphibian." In *Wikipedia*, March 13, 2023. https://en.wikipedia.org/w/index.php?title=Amphibian&oldid=1144394264

- Animals. "Mexican Axolotl," March 1, 2014. https://kids.nationalgeographic.com/animals/amphibians/facts/mexican-axolotl

- Blue Reef Aquarium. "What Is an Axolotl and Why Are They Endangered?," October 30, 2020. https://www.bluereefaquarium.co.uk/portsmouth/blog/education/what-is-an-axolotl-and-why-are-they-endangered/

- "Can I House Two Axolotls Together? Will They Fight? – Water Critters," March 19, 2018. https://www.watercritters.ca/2018/03/19/can-i-house-two-axolotls-together-will-they-fight/

- Consulting, Serendipit. "Five Axolotl Fun Facts About a Fascinating Aquatic Pet." AZPetVet, May 2, 2022. https://www.azpetvet.com/five-axolotl-fun-facts-about-a-fascinating-aquatic-pet/

- gb_dev. "Making Difficult Decisions for Your Pet." The Animal Medical Center, June 7, 2010. https://www.amcny.org/blog/2010/06/07/making-difficult-decisions-for-your-pet/

- H, Jess. "6 Fun Accessories for an Axolotl Tank." PetHelpful, March 31, 2023 https://pethelpful.com/reptiles-amphibians/6-Fun-Accessories-for-an-Axolotl-Tank

- Hall, Heather. "Axolotl Lifespan: How Long Do They Live?" AZ Animals, October 16, 2021. https://a-z-animals.com/blog/axolotl-lifespan-how-long-do-they-live/

- "How to Care for an Axolotl: 10 Steps (with Pictures) - WikiHow." https://www.wikihow.com/Care-for-an-Axolotl

- https://www.facebook.com/aquariumstoredepot. "Axolotl Tank Mates - 5 Suitable (and 4 Bad Ones!) - AquariumStoreDepot," November 16, 2021. https://aquariumstoredepot.com/blogs/news/axolotl-tank-mates

- https://www.facebook.com/thesprucepets. "Keeping and Caring for Axolotls as Pets." The Spruce Pets. https://www.thesprucepets.com/axolotls-as-pets-1236714

- Kellyville Pets. "How to Look after an Axolotl." https://www.kellyvillepets.com.au/pages/how-to-look-after-an-axolotl

- National Geographic. "Amphibian Pictures & Facts." https://www.nationalgeographic.com/animals/amphibians

- . "What Is the Life Cycle of An Axolotl?" *Pets From Afar* (blog). https://petsfromafar.com/axolotl-life-cycle/

- Nerd, Axolotl. "Axolotls Growth Stages and Growth Rate." Axolotl Nerd, October 24, 2020. https://axolotlnerd.com/axolotls-growth-stages-rate/

- "Pick a Pet." Accessed May 23, 2023. https://www.decision-making-solutions.com/pick-a-pet.html

- prezi.com. "Axolotl Life Cycle." Accessed May 23, 2023. https://prezi.com/lx5d1to5_jfr/axolotl-life-cycle/

- Ross, Heather. "Axolotl Colors: The 10 Types of Axolotl Morphs." AZ Animals, January 17, 2022. https://a-z-animals.com/blog/axolotl-colors-the-10-types-of-axolotl-morphs/

- The Tye-Dyed Iguana - Reptiles and Reptile Supplies in St. Louis. "How to Keep Your Exotic Pet Happy: Amphibian Edition." Accessed May 23, 2023. https://thetyedediguana.com/blog/how-to-keep-your-exotic-pet-happy-amphibian-edition/

- "Underwater Camouflage." In *Wikipedia*, May 12, 2023. https://en.wikipedia.org/w/index.php?title=Underwater_camouflage&oldid=1154374330

- We Know Pets. "Thinking About Getting an Axolotl? Here's What You Need to Know to Make an Informed Decision," March 2, 2023. https://www.weknowpets.com.au/blogs/news/thinking-about-getting-an-axolotl-heres-what-you-need-to-know-to-make-an-informed-decision

- "What You Need to Know Before Buying Fish." https://www.petplace.com/article/fish/general/what-you-need-to-know-before-buying-fish/

Printed in Great Britain
by Amazon

25994164R00051